FORMELESS

Poetry

Raïs Neza Boneza

Mwanaka Media and Publishing Pvt Ltd,
Chitungwiza, Zimbabwe
*

Creativity, Wisdom, and Beauty

Publisher: *Mmap*
Mwanaka Media and Publishing Pvt Ltd
24 Svosve Road, Zengeza 1
Chitungwiza, Zimbabwe

mwanaka@yahoo.commwanaka13@gmail.com
https://www.mmapublishing.org
www.africanbookscollective.com/publishers/mwanaka-media-and-publishing
https://facebook.com/MwanakaMediaAndPublishing/

Distributed in and outside N. America by African Books Collective
orders@africanbookscollective.com
www.africanbookscollective.com

ISBN: 978-1-77931-484-0
EAN: 9781779314840

Print: Libri Plureos GmbH, Friedensallee 273, 22763 Hamburg, Germany

DISCLAIMER

All views expressed in this publication are those of the author and do not necessarily reflect the views of *Mmap*.

INDEX

INDEX

INDEX

Introduction: Raïs Neza Boneza's Poetry Odyssey

In the realm of poetic brilliance, where words effortlessly transcend their earthly bounds, Raïs Neza Boneza stands as a multilingual virtuoso, enchanting readers with the mastery of language and imagery. Boneza's poetic prowess is like a shape-shifting entity, evoking emotions and thoughts that defy conventional form and structure.

In "Formless," Boneza's latest poetry collection, the reader is invited to embark on an odyssey through the boundless realms of the human soul. These verses, like shapeless apparitions, materialize from the depths of Boneza's creative spirit, transcending the limitations of traditional poetry. In this enigmatic journey, Boneza invites us to explore the limitless possibilities of language and the malleable nature of human emotions.

Within the verses of "Formless," a haunting melancholy lingers, a reflection of the profound hopelessness that often plagues the human condition. The poet's introspective musings challenge us to confront the inherent flaws in human nature and beckon us to initiate change, urging us to take responsibility for the choices that shape our lives.

Time, an ever-present specter, weaves its indelible presence throughout the collection, a reminder of its ceaseless march and the ephemeral nature of existence. Love, too, is a recurring theme, celebrated and yearned for, an emotion that transcends the boundaries of form and substance.

As you immerse yourself in the formless beauty of Boneza's verses, you will embark on an odyssey through the kaleidoscope of human experience. "Formless" is a testament to the boundless potential of language and the enigmatic depths of the human spirit. These verses, like ethereal whispers, will linger in your consciousness, inviting you to explore the complexities of existence and the timeless power of poetry.

End to humanity ´s schism

Let's put an end to the disolution of humanity,
so that bombing and massacres cease,
and peace can come where it has been brutally removed
Let's put an end to the division of humanity,
so that the endless bombing
of the helpless and migrants may come to an end,
hungry and punished for daring,
o seek a bit of lost freedom.

They are not responsible for your daily words.
They did not cause your precariousness.
They did not take away your jobs or increase your taxes.
They did not ask your representatives to fund deadly conflicts around the world.
They did not provoke wars at your borders.
Let us remember the guillotines for those guilty of these crimes.

Let's go, put an end to humanity disarray.
so that lands, oceans,
to rivers and mountains, deserts, and forests,
from south to north,
from sunrise to sunset,
so that these places may nurture the original consciousness.

Let's put an end to the division of humanity
so that terms like
slavery and crime against humanity
do not vanish in the sterile speeches of good intentions.
Let's put an end to the division of humanity,
so that healing and dignity may come
with solidarity.

For this world, whose division
has fueled serial genocides
from the earlier centuries to the present day,
rooted in the provoked disappearance of indigenous peoples in America,
Australia's Aboriginals,
Namibia's Hereros,
Auschwitz's human furnace,

the horror of Nanking,
the firestorms of Hiroshima and Nagasaki,
the Cambodian genocide,
the Rwandan pogrom,
to the silent genocide from the Congo to Palestine.

May this schism come to an end,
may the sly and silent wars cease,
may the division through genetic manipulation
to weakened humanity cease.

May these words
bear witness to the
voices that have risen,
that are rising, and will continue to rise against
the annihilation of humanity.

Today, relentlessly, voices cry out
to the technologically deafened ears
of the descendants of those
who punish the world
for aspiring to the ideal of freedom.

May these verbs
be the guardians of humanity's conscience,
so that the words
resound the almost extinguished light emanating
from the pen for a return
to an empathic altruism.

Let's put an end to the dismemberment of humanity,
so that a bit of humanity finds its place
in this troubled world.
Is it not time to heal the ancestral wounds
that dictate global slavery today,
that lead to the fragmentation of humanity
with all the necessary humanitarian precautions
in these times when every effort is made
to erase the gains of shared knowledge
in the depths of a memory catastrophe.

Nightfall's Mirror

The darkness within the gaze
solstice of wrath
when bravery
strolls, withers, slithers
nips the dirt.
When spirits ceremoniously parade,
they dance to the tune of every crackling,
whether it's the unwanted memories
or the shattered prophecies.

Unable to find its symbol of faith
and failing to uncover a refuge,
unable to overcome doubt.

In the gloomy depths of understanding,
the skies within one's eyes release tearful sobs,
critiquing with a flowing stream of regret.

The star in the eyes
radiance of the world
contemplates its tale
in flames of ridicule.

The duskiness eyesight
clings to the drops of time
because the earth's saddles
dissolve like salt
in the fare of the present moment.

Star Reverie

I am gazing at the Milky Way, stars' remnants so bright,
I find wonder in the cosmic tale of the night.
The wind carries hope through the quiet expanse,
Its heart gently beating in a tranquil dance.

A fairy, bathed in the moon's icy gleam,
reflects upon her essence in the tranquil dream.
The wind, a gentle whisperer in the frosty air,
as the world surrenders to sleep, without a care.

In the still slumber, silence holds its sway,
an illusory choir of memories at play.
longing for a sunset to stir the heart's fire,
a fairy dreams as the darkness climbs higher.

Drifting in shadows, the day bids goodbye,
a gentle mirror, where the soul can't deny.
The Milky Way, a vast cosmic tapestry's grace,
whispers stories of time, memories embrace.

Yearning

I've ceased to be just me, I long to be only like you,
to feel how deeply my heart and body yearn for you;
what does it mean to be alone? For me, we're meant to be,
Without you, I'm barren ground, where bitterness is free;

Each morning, I'm reborn, a new self, don't you see?
For every night, death takes a piece of me,
Without you, I'm adrift, with no law or decree;
To revive us, my love, what's the key that sets us free?

Samaria

In the name of God and the land, they say with such grace,
Hell yes! What a feast for a dark and twisted place.
Today, when we speak against the specter of death,
We are painted as fanatics, losing our collective breath.

Those who profess to teach the lofty rights of humanity's dream,
claim to bear the torch of international law, it may seem.
Now, they choose to arm those who've shown,
a knack for taking lives at random, with no remorse,
the fires of hate, colonization and genocides on its course.

Let's extinguish this fire that engulfs a nation's soul,
when we kill so efficiently, it's the devil's own goal.
O! Samaria, lives are lost, just like yours and mine,
innocent souls trapped in violence's endless grind.

How do we fight horror without becoming its face?
Let's open a path to a humane embrace.
Eh! Perhaps a humanitarian corridor, a glimmer of light,
For peace brutally removed, why not parley with those who fight?

Judah burns with no consequences, Eh! he is powerful and bold,
While the gods and the world, in silence, withhold.
When we master the art of killing in God's holy name,
Hell is just a carnival, a twisted, tragic game.

Taking lives in the name of a god, with unwavering scorn,
leaves nothing for the devil, who's forlorn and worn.
Perhaps God is on leave, as the world's steeped in sin,
but every life has value, regardless of the faith within.

Again yes! every child holds worth,
then, let's end this tragedy, extinguish horror's hearth.
The infernal flames of suffering,
let's quell,
For all lives matters, in this world where we dwell.

The Night Whisperer

I write to escape from the shadows,
from despair, from discouragement,
when the sun's escape,
when the intoxication of sleep,
when the night awakens me,
I feel the words panicking in the dark.

Like a drum rolling in my head.
Like the embrace of the torrent,
squeezing me to the core of my soul.

So, even if I'm asleep,
it's in the night that I write,
it's in the night that I bite,
it's in the night that I awake,
it's in the night that I paint,
the pains of my life,
with the magic that slips away.

The bit in my teeth to go faster,
the night is my escape,
Yet, it's there that I reside.
Dreams and awakenings that touch,
Those of days that rise and set,
Those of bodies that intertwine and entwine.

The dance of self-discovery

In the quest for self-discovery, I wander,
Navigating uncharted waters with wonder.
Motivation, a wild and untamed wind,
No strings attached, no games to rescind.

No second-guessing, no crystal ball,
Just hopes, answering my inner call.
In the echoes of my expectations,
A solo dance of hopeful aspirations.

Numbness, a shield from life's occasional pain,
Yet courage says, "Feel it, don't abstain."
To feel is to tango with the fiery flame,
A daring dance in life's unpredictable game.

Find peace, seeker, in the tranquil glen,
Elevate your spirit, let it transcend.
The journey is a canvas, a living art,
Paint it with the hues of your brave heart.

Untitled

Aching yet profound,
Find solace, imbibe insight,
Endure, assimilate.

Untitled

Humans crave for meaning,
Paradox in every step,
Divided, yet bound.

Seeking significance,
Paradox in our essence,
Divisive, yet fundamentally one.

Frontline

On a battlefield, the ink cries its plea,
In our arena where struggles, we constantly see.
With hopes as armor, dreams take their flight,
Yet doubts sneak in through the cover of night.

Weighted by self-doubt, comparisons we wear,
Valor and bravery leave their marks to bear.
It's not just about winning, as struggles unfold,
But in learning, we find treasures untold.

Paper shares stories of every skirmish and fray,
In the dance of progress, we find our own way.
Our battles etched in each written line,
A narrative of growth, a sign of our own design.

Breeze of Influence

A piece of history's legacy,
roots fading into the depths of time,
an old saying repeats, its origins but a mystery.

Jesus, Hitler, and the pandemics intersect,
A peculiar convergence in the labyrinth of thought,
A trio of disparate influences, disquieting.

Mind and programming intertwine,
Crafting thoughts, shaping actions,
A complex waltz with hidden threads.

Curious, the potency of influence,
In the corridors of cognition,
Where echoes of past and present interlace.

Grief

Oh! No
What else remains...?
In the wake of sadness,
The loss of a dear soul,
A sharp blow deep within,
In times of drought,
Smiles in a heart that withers,
Like this pain that dries up,
The joy of living, the pleasure of surviving,
Amid life's blows and its wounds.

No,
What else remains...?
In the grip of despair,
All the dreams of the soul,
Shattered and scattered,
Streaming like rain,
When the promises of a verdant dawn,
Fade day by day,
And the night suffocates the day,
Yesterday condemns tomorrow,
To live endlessly the same way of life.

Oh no.
What else remains...?
In the face of failure,
When love loses its taste,
Faced with a sense of helplessness,
And life's sorrows
rage against existence,
Sweeping away all hope of life,
The future clings to escaping,
One day from misery's grip,
For those whose hearts
hold the concern to see their happiness bloom.

Lured by Light

Drawn to the flame, captivated by its glow,
A shake with brilliance, a yearning to know.
Intrigued, attaching to the radiant beam,
Vibrant wings flutter within a luminous dream.

Soaring freely, in shades unspoken,
Gliding on winds, a story woven.
Winds of transformation, whispers unchained,
Yet, in the charm's sweetness, I'm named.

Like honey, sticky and sweet,
Ensnared by allure, in charm's heartbeat.
Intelligence weaves a complex thread,
A delicate dance where illusions are spread.

In the fragile balance of light and night,
I navigate realms, a creature taking flight.
A moth to the flame, a timeless connection,
In the adhesive embrace, a lesson's reflection.

Shades of Doubt

In the system we've embraced,
I strive, though doubts leave traces.
With sunglasses on, tinted with query,
Morning affirmation seeks soul's sanctuary.

"Release doubts and fears," it gently urges,
Resonating in the mind as uncertainty surges.
Yet, my shades retain a lingering hue,
Morning glints with remnants of doubt too.

"I am safe," the mantra's comforting grace,
A shield against shadows, a secure place.
In the labyrinth of programmed thought,
I navigate, seeking clarity.

A move with doubts, a morning's trial,
In our chosen system, a heartfelt mile.
To release the doubts, embrace what's near,
In the sunlight's warmth, let go of fear.

Tropic buzz

Beneath tropical suns, where colors come alive,
A crimson envelope holds stories, ancient and wise.
Prosperity murmurs amid the rustling trees,
Luck and virtue undulate in the tropical breeze.

In the heart of Asia and African terrains,
Dragon's roar, tiger's prowl, in nature's domains.
Quiet murmurs within the lush undergrowth,
Whispers of secrets, a symphony of oaths.

The dense foliage hides tales yet to be told,
Heard for miles, in the tropics' gentle hold.
A blend of cultures, under the equatorial sway,
Nature's canvas painted in daylight's array.

Riding thoughts

Avoiding the stage of conflict, drama's reprieve,
I step aside, escaping the tense narrative weave.
Toxic utterances, manipulations of speech,
I evade them in silence's distant reach.

Mental projections, a cinematic display,
Monkey mind's magic, on clouds it finds its way.
Riding the skies like a celestial steed,
In boundless space, where thoughts intercede.

No puppeteer's strings, just the mind's ballet,
A dance on clouds, in the light of day.
Resistant to drama's snare, ensnaring,
I hover above, in the rarified air I'm sharing.

Harmonize with the sacred,
Life's journey, a thrill ride,
Crests and troughs collide.
Velocity and unease entwine,
Thrill and anxiety combine.

Swiging thougths

Am I question's echo?
Doubt dances in fleeting steps,
Consistency craved.
Yet, I change like clouds at play,
Ever-shifting, a dance each day.

The unspoken

Urgency, a quiet, coiled force,
Bottled anticipation, secrets held off course.
Passions simmer, day and night,
Fantasies weaving in concealed light.

A yearning, a weight like a handbag's tote,
Carried gracefully in life's daily yoke.
Unbridled desires, a flame untamed,
In the heart's theater, no name to be named.

Embers of longing, a fire held in check,
Outlined against the night's soft silhouette.
Urgency whispers, an unyielding plea,
In the dance of desires, wild and free.

In the shadows of camaraderie, thoughts concealed,
Are we bound in a cult or love revealed?
A love bomb explodes, hope takes flight,
Promises of a brighter future, a path so bright.

Dancing in the radiant glow of self-esteem,
No space for doubt, no burdensome theme.
In the cult of confidence, we find our way,
A journey where self-love guides each day.

Growing up

In our childhood, our primary goal was to survive,
and we were in a constant state of change and growth,
not content with staying the same.
We looked up to the adults as our guides
and trusted their actions to teach us valuable lessons.

Our behaviors were like a blank canvas,
ready to be shaped and defined.
However, as we grew older,
we quickly realized that reality was not a smooth path
but rather a turbulent ride.

Our experiences were like messy drafts,
filled with scribbles and uncertainties,
and life itself was the school
where we learned important lessons.

Just like fish in a river,
we adapted to the changing currents,
sometimes swimming against the flow
and other times going with the rapids.

We faced the choice of settling into the challenges
or putting in all our effort to overcome them.
As children, we learned to navigate the darkest moments of our lives,
and this journey we call life was an ongoing spectacle.
Growing up made us aware of how our own stories would continue to evolve.

Whispers of the Drum

Audible whispers, the stolen speech's embrace,
Trapped in hallucinations, reality's misplaced grace.
People entered, their presence transient,
Never to return, a mystery inherent.

Awake or asleep, the line blurs,
I beat my drum, where rhythms begin.
In the realm of dreams, syncopation's gleam,
A dance of echoes, a silent scream.

Ripples of acoustic tales gently unfurl,
Vibrations of change, a story to swirl.
Within the drumbeats, a language profound,
A symphony of silence, a surreal sound.

Blood and Bonds

Blood and water, you see, it's in our veins,
Chromosomes connecting, it's in our chains.
Family features, traits that define,
Temperament and personalities, in the design.

Focus and intention, within the family brew,
Hidden history, unsaid experiences, it's true.
Through a child's eyes, innocence beheld,
Tainted, groomed, by kindness or resentment held.

We might not always vibe, not in every zone,
Yet, connected by blood, by bones we're known.
Synchronicity in the random meets,
Fleeting moments, life's rhythmic beats.

Not locked into patterns, breaking free,
In the dance of life, that's where will be.
Freedom's a choice, not a sentence in chains,
In the poetry of life, blood and bones remain.

Birthing

In the umbilical code,
we're nurtured for nine months,
and then we're born,
unfolding into the world.
Our origins,
once hidden,
are now revealed

Untitled

Competition's drive,
Survival sparks,
seeking our thrive,
Ambition awakened.

Embracing Life's Flow

Adapting to life,
expectations or spontaneous strife,
you can navigate,
no need for resentment or debate.

Release all judgment's hold,
let each path, its own story unfold.

Dawn

Dawn breaks,
with subtle meditation,
observing the natural mystic,
bandwidth tuned to a frequency,
with no static.

Dawn approaches
I'm already awake,
visualising
what can I accomplish for the day.

And sunlight
morning meditation.
waking up to birdsound
and neighbours
trying to be discreet from their nakedness

now I'm awake
smelling insense for the day.

African Resilience: a poetical manifesto

As we rise above, we persist, we're the best.
Be cautious at the boundaries you seek,
Before they close, before the stories retreat,
Beside the good, evil sometimes hides,
Beyond them, tears and grudges may speak.
Both play their roles on life's winding tides.
Broken hearts and wounds, both bitter and deep,

But bigger and blacker
But we choose to break free with creativity
But we forged our path, and come what may.
But we're alive, and that's something rare.
But we're still here, our strength reassured.
Creating beauty, creativity, and what we project to be.

Don't judge by appearances, just take a look,
Enter into our hearts, don't delay,
Enter our hearts, where stories begin,
Fear not the shadows that haunt our night,
Followed by deserved reparations, I fear.
For it won't come overseas, that the truth to embrace.
For our art is the testament of our eternal youth.
For society often demands conformity,
For we're here to make things beautiful and bold,

In a world that's often lost its way.
In defiance of those who wished us away,
In every color, creed, and every face.

In our hearts, beyond the facade's art,
In our hearts, where emotions take flight,
In silent repose, the truth you'll find,
In the pages of life, where our stories unfurl,
In these chambers of love, our souls shall meet.
In these sacred chambers, where we dare to dream.
In this world, we won't be the same.

Innocence lost since our youth,
Intoxicated by dreams, in the day and night.
Intoxicated by love, they shine so bright.
Joy dwells here, free from sorrow's chains.
Know that our hearts are filled with delight,
Let us heal, bend, and make our space real,
Lie treasures unseen, in every part.

Listen closely to the whispers of your mind.
Losing ourselves in a book, we find our own dream.
Love's roses bloom, but beware, there's more than oneself.
Make the gesture of faith, endeavor to be clever.
Mysteries abound, as we look within.
Mysterious chambers, like books on a shelf,
No explanation for the cruelty endured,
Not just blood courses through these veins,

O! Africa, bigger and blacker
O! Africa, let us embrace our grace,
One day, we'll conquer them with love's pure light.
Our dreams flourish, in every direction they gleam,
Our humanity, we proudly re-claim,
Self-healing, it's our daunting quest,

Sometimes,
Stay with me here, where our secrets hide.
That fills every corner, every sacred space.
The door is but a glimpse of the worlds we forsook.
The doors of our hearts, they won't stand forever,
The poet's not mad, it's poetry's sweet grace,
They're open wide, where dreams hold sway.
To speak for all humankind and generation to come.

We discover ourselves, as we lose in a swirl.
We may never hear any true apologies
We must leave behind families, countries, and more..
We pretend to be less as our true selves is denied.
We shine bright, unapologetically, every single day.

we stand here today,
We testify to our existence, bold and free,
We understand these hidden corners, we reside,
We're the voices of change, resilience, and truth,
With no support, no guidance, no clear way,
Within the pages of life's complex scheme,
Witness to a legacy of madness and despair,
Yet our hearts still find their own special ways.

Beneath the Surface

Deep waters, like midnight's cloak,
silhouettes of insomnia, secrets spoken,
posted for posterity, a record stark,
polar bears dancing in the dark.

Deep waters, akin to layered onions,
refracted light's depths, like suns.
Optical illusions, not what they seem,
mirages of assumptions, a fleeting dream.

Take time to sense the silent intention,
Trust your intuition, a guide's ascension.

Healing

Discharging,
Releasing negative emotional weight.
Freedom blossoms from past wounds' trauma.
Muscle testing clears, fasting catharsis as armor.
Acknowledging the inner child's plea for compassion.
Yet impatience still lingers, a fleeting reaction.

A spirit yearning to mend an unresolved void,
in remembrance of a youthful period tainted with shame.

Embrace Your Power

She told me not to care,
those people aren't important, don't despair.
they're teaching you a lesson, it's clear,
What is it? You're more than they'll ever hear.

Their subtle innuendo speaks, it's true,
Turn up the volume, let your strength shine through.
Don't get distracted by the distortion's art,
Remember, the ears never close, play your part.

Don't wait for miracles, let your dreams take flight,
Create your destiny, wield your own might.
You have agency, so boldly embrace,
Look into your eyes and affirm, "I am enough," with grace.

Don't waste your bandwidth, don't drift about,
Tune in and tune out, find your inner route.
Carve out the angel in the marble, be free,
Embrace your power, let your true self be.

Navigating Earthly Realms

Down to earth,
I ponder my worth,
Do I truly desire to be grounded?
Terrestrial attachments, the matrix, astounded.

We often feel out of sync, out of line,
with a life that seems standard, defined.
Elephant-like, I sense through my feet,
subtle vibrations, memories to greet.

Like the soul of black folk, generations flow,
My challenge is clear, to be here, to grow.
To stay present amidst life's fleeting dance,
In the earthly realm, find my true stance.

Embracing the Depths

Embrace the darkness,
glistening with residue of denial.
In time, I shall emerge bathed in the radiant light of clarity,
no shame, just a profound acceptance of my identity,
loyalty, ever vigilant, prepared for the battle ahead.

Emotional bandwidth,
like deep waters, with icebergs and tides so grand,
flowing around the sphere of self, an endless expanse,
navigating personal odysseys, taking a chance,
charting the coordinates of our inner lands.

The Mighty Caravan

Endings are beginnings, the spirit serpent says,
take solace, dear souls, in life's intricate shifts,
no accidents here, destiny's plan softly drifts.
In the mind, the mighty caravan's story unfolds,
each chapter, a secret, the universe beholds.

Yes, in this modern age we find technology aids,
yet intention, the driving force, in the soul entwined.
All is well, trust the path, the journey revealing,
the mighty caravan of life, its secrets concealing.

Formless Journey

The path of evolution is distinct for each one,
as in life's intricate tapestry,
each person plays a vital role.

Embrace this voyage,
make it your very own,
for it's a path that is ever-changing
and yet beautifully unknown.
Let the journey take shape in its formlessness

Reclaiming Oneself

I release limiting beliefs, set them free,
born from the scars of wars and past memory.
I witness toxic politics, a never-ending game,
generations chained, repeating lies without shame.

When we delete the old program's hold,
defrag the motherboard, create new stories untold,
no longer captive to the virus we spurn,
feeding the beast with falsehoods, lessons learned.

The allure of grand illusions, charming and sly,
masked as humility with intricate layers, oh my!
like treacle tart and sweet maple syrup's gleam,
I no longer claim them as part of my dream.

Embracing past influence, with a knowing heart,
I can reshape the patterns, a brand-new start.
Alone yet strong, I find my way,
safe, excited, manifesting each day.

With clear intention, I create my own theme,
deleting old programs, like a fresh, vibrant dream.
no longer shackled by what came before,
I've rebooted my system, forevermore.

Filtering Life's Layers

Filtering out the debris, the outdated and worn,
Slowing life's pace at each red light we've torn.
Choosing left or right, yet still in the flow we stay,
Navigating the journey, come what may.

Happy moments in others we see,
Seeking external joy, contentment's decree.
Craving acceptance and inner peace's embrace,
Yet, for many the healing will not arrive in this lifetime.

I listen to myself with intent and grace,
attuning to the words, the wisdom we embrace.
Like a tuning fork that resonates true,
I learn to trust the vibrations, as I grew.

Unrushed Growth

Sometimes we try to force the river's flow,
rushing towards success, we want to go.
Thinking time is scarce, we hurry and strive,
Yet, if we took a moment, we'd truly come alive.

Incubate ourselves, trust the unfolding scheme,
Embrace the process, learn from each dream.
Without anxiety, do our best with grace,
We can be more than expectations we face.

One ´s odyssey

Raw, limitless integration unfolds,
Absorbing into the pool of existence, as life molds.
Without identity, yet far from frivolous,
Flexible, compassionate, patient, life's compass.

In uncharted waters, I find my way,
flowing steadily, listening to what the heart might say.
Taking responsibility for each decision, I discern,
slash and burn doubts, embrace my uniqueness in turn.

Frustration's real, but endurance is the call,
Even when others place their foot upon us.
In the futuristic frequency of days gone by,
A play I wrote, of connection that could defy.

Tuned into the Akashic record's eternal hum,
Timeless, evolving, a story yet to become.
Rebellious, not stubborn, living outside the box,
Peering into Pandora's containment, with paradox.

Through hell or high water, blame is but a game,
Responsibility takes humility, a different aim.
Shame seeks ego, supremacy finds its kin,
War needs enemies, while peace breeds within.

Compromise hungers for equality's embrace,
Justice requires acknowledgement of deeds, done or to face

Nights

Dark night, where flowers rest in silence,
Where azure skies and daytime sounds retire,
A night for pleasure and forgetting,
Resting by the shores of Tanganyika,
In the quiet dark, the soul stirs and dreams.

O eternal night, source of profound quiet,
Whisper to my heart with a gentle sea breeze,
Like a flower swaying to love's sweet call,
Illuminate my owl-like eyes, sleepless night!

You, who watch us with starry eyes above,
See my heart racing, like a ship's mast in storm,
Breaking and flapping with every gust.

Dark night, like the skin's deep embrace,
Your hair, like foam from the calm sea's face,
In the midst of the abyss, beyond all borders,
You bring silence, without dreams or disorder.

Night, you birth sounds in the depths of silence,
Voices tangled, a lamentation of souls.
It's the voice of my hopes, the voice of my tears.

Traveling night, companion of countless spirits,
Go, awaken my sacred desires,
Remain gentle within me, embrace my soul.

I despise the dawn, with its sorrows and strife,
It dims my words and burdens my songs.
But you, night, eternal and ideal,
Watch over my confused stars with a tender seal.

O dark night, cradler of my dreams and delights!

Ballade quest

In life, I've learned that humans often act selfishly,
Survival's standard practice, though others may be involved partly.
Rare but possible, the exchange of giving and receiving,
I ache inside, not wanting to, but I can't stop believing.

I see you through rose-colored glasses, tainted by regret,
Acknowledging the duality, the fish and the twin, we mustn't forget.
Mystical truths defy logic, study the energy of this pair,
Duality's part of manifestation, complementary, not in comparison's snare.

From zero, it all originates, peace and elevation combined,
A servant to the light, not blinded by truth's glare, I'm defined.
My optics remain open, no shroud of rose-colored glass,
Translucent radiance and potential to feel safe, within us, we amass.

I am an oasis of peace and safety, come sit or rest a while,
Embrace the love with no expectations, let authenticity beguile.
Shed the pretense the monkey mind inhabits, relax, be still,
An epilogue not yet finished, intuition strong, my truth to fulfill.

Should I heed the opinions of those in denial, in supposed morality's name?
Authentic, soft but not weak, nurturing, generous, in my flame.
Firm but honest, yielding, flexible, I can bend and float on a breeze,
Weightless and challenged, bearing traumas and fatigue with ease.
On this journey with no distance, can we travel together, if you dare?
But if not, I'm content to travel alone, appreciating your company,
Arriving at the pearly gates, dreaming of heaven, sequins and jasper's hue.

For my heart to be weighed, lighter than a feather, I pray,
Wondering what I did with my liberty, my life's display.
Yet, I can't quite put my finger on it, feeling change's pulse within,
A skeptic at heart, I may be, but my voice deserves to begin.

If you have security, you're allowed an opinion to share,
I may not always agree, but I promise to listen with care.
Disengaging my compassion, my heart soft but not weak,

Kindness doesn't mean I'm powerless;
strength is what I'll speak.

Legacy isn't my wish as the body turns to dust,
With weakened muscles, I reflect on death and life's trust.
Becoming light, not dense, in the journey's embrace,
Dreaming of old friends, longing for a special place.

The ego seeks attention, the center of life's stage,
Visiting me daily, I laugh, like one in dementia's cage.
But it's not funny, this blend of rooibos tea and honey's embrace,
Succulent aroma, tingling senses, a sweet and pungent grace.

I realize I deserve to be happy, no more fighting for acceptance,
I deserve to be honored, questioning life's essence.
Diligently seeking the best, no compromise in my quest,
I am worth it all, and I'll continue to be my best.

Remanent echoes

I had a friend, an artistic soul,
Always in a whirl, yet a genius whole,
Yes, we held her dear,
I cherished her near,
In a hostel room, we found her plight,
Overdosed and gone, a pale, sad light;

I knew this old man
An amateur politician with a plan,
He went to his home late, always drank in the mornings
For the smallest of strife,
He hurt his wife, made her sink,
Yes, we cared for him in life,
But in death's embrace, he lay so stark,
In the booze's dark depths, forever marked.

I had an uncle, Vegar was his name,
In unemployment, he found no shame,
With a degree in hand, luck smiled upon him
He held his head high, the town hall extended its hand to him
He was punctual, we liked him that way
He was too honest, some hated him for it
But I liked him well
I held him dear through thick and thin,
He had a bloated belly, I was by his bedside
He had ashen skin, I read his farewells!

I had a neighbor, André, a sight to see,
Rastafarian style, not always free,
A bit racist, always filled with spite,
Locked up, day and night,
Sometimes social, sometimes alone,
In paranoia, he'd often groan,
Yet we cared for him, it's true,
And I did too, more than a few,

In the emergency room, he met his end,
Leaving behind a wound that won't mend;
I can hardly believe it.

I knew Abdullaziz, top of his class,
A perfectionist with vast ambition,
Shining like the eastern sun,
We liked him
I liked him too
But an inconvenient witness, he became,
In a web of deceit, and a dangerous game,
The other day, we found him beneath the bridge, his life ceased,
In the shadow of suspicion, his life was leased;

I had a colleague in the west,
Self-diagnosed and on a spiritual quest,
Yet unstable, never at rest,
Consulting gurus and all kind of shaman
Swallowing potions, reciting mantras,
In her search for meaning, she was strong,
Everyone held her in esteem,
And I, too, cherished her dream,
But in the end, she faced her fight,
Radiation's toll, a dimming light,
She hung her apron, paid the cost,
And now I too fear, my life may be lost.

Voyage

The path of life is an intricate tapestry, woven with lessons and insights, each moment a thread in the grand design. If you stumble, rise again, embracing humility and grace even when it feels uncomfortable. None of us can be right all the time, but that doesn't diminish our worth.

The law of gravity reminds us that what goes up must come down, a universal truth mirrored in the ebb and flow of our experiences. Embrace discomfort, not in squalor or meager conditions, but in recognizing our abundance. Humility, though challenging, is a pursuit found even in the scriptures.

The legacy of societal "isms" lurks in plain sight, camouflaged for safety, seeping into our subconscious, justifying our positions. Taking risks and baring vulnerabilities can be daunting, but true growth lies in facing fears head-on.

Life, akin to menopause or puberty, unfolds with hormonal shifts, disrupting sleep patterns and offering clarity amid weight gain. Navigating through ego darkness requires heart-centered struggles, steering clear of rampant miscommunication and illusory comparisons.

Love, a quality that expands the chest, is eternal, extending beyond commercialized celebrations. Inner knowledge helps release past pain, fostering a sense of abundance. Managing oneself, avoiding herding by immunity, acknowledges differences while rejecting fear-based protection.

Taking chances and risking something rather than settling for all or nothing leads to growth. Meanings change over time, words carry power, but their meanings evolve, contributing to our collective confusion. Measure time by consciousness, embrace synchronicity, and let intention guide actions.

In the merry march of life, stepping in rotation, formation emerges with springtime colors, bursting with sap and ready for new life after slumbering in darkness. Moments, captured or recorded, speak volumes, but memories may blur over time, causing us to question their reality.

Moonbeams shower light in the dark, revealing emotions nurtured in childhood shadows. Liberation lies in the acknowledgment that change is possible, and feeling worthy is acceptable. More love layered atop abundance expands the heart, evoking tears of joy.

Morning breezes and distant traffic heard through open windows, midnight messages read in tealight candlelight - these simple moments contribute to the symphony of life. Homeostasis and biodiversity, like natural selection, raise questions about strength, flexibility, and adaptability.

Loss, rather than being mourned, can be seen as an opportunity. Predictability is an illusion; freedom lies in embracing the unknown. Love, as a quality, causes the chest to expand, filled with the vapors of acceptance, tingling feelings, and radiant joy.

In a world filled with complexities, simplicity becomes a treasure. The heaviness of overthinking contrasts with the simplicity of meal prep, though even that can be confusing at times. The silent, troubled pumpkin eater carries a weight that echoes through the silent funeral procession.

Insight differs from mainstream opinions, making people nervous when confronted with "otherness." Loss, a personal storm, brings forth the glare of clarity. Silence becomes a comforting blanket, urging stillness in the face of death.

Inherited traits, like nitpicking, present choices - perpetuating a cycle or choosing compassion and self-acceptance to showcase the beauty of communal support.

Some family dynamics can be toxic and judgmental. Drawing invisible lines around one's aura separates personal truths from external judgments. Placing the creator at the center, not oneself, challenges conditioning from family, society, and the silent majority. Becoming a new being involves releasing ancestral conditioning, realizing that nothing is truly new under the sun.

The voyage continues, navigating through the intricacies of life, choosing growth over stagnation, and finding solace in the timeless wisdom passed down through generations.

Jazz

Hi mate, follow me
look up, see how blue and beautiful the firmament is
lower your eyes
see how much the trees foliage dance in harmony.
We can read the joy from their rhythmic folly.

Be my guest, lets go up to the last floor
admire the fixed architecture of our city
in space and time.
Feel the wind blowing on your face.

Now my visitor gets into your heart
see how much my heart is like a bird
flutters, happy to probe the beauty
inside your azure.
He poses on the summits
of your trees,
one after the other
appreciating them all.
And resumes his flight,
he flies over the spaces
between your buildings,
his wings draw melodic notes:
happy tunes,
harmonious sounds
black and white.

Are they confused?

The Jazz
where my heart
and your heart
describe one after another
the beautiful fusion
where the viola and the solo
merge.

Where the soprano and the bass
make a harmonious rule.

Go ahead my song because it is sweet
our confusion is law, and
our only law is confusion.
Let's go my tango
O! beauty,
O! sweetness.
Go again my splendor.

Dewdrop ´Lessons

Sweet dew,
Not constrained by the matrix.
Rain pours as libation,
And the empty gourd fills with water.
Taking risks,
Can be daunting,
If fear takes hold.
Be fearless, unapologetic,
mistakes don't mean the end of the world,
acceptance doesn't require remorse.
Kindness is a choice, not a chore,
and compassion acknowledges our losses.
Tall glasses,
Filled with glistening crystals,
Ice cubes catching the light,
Melting, diluting the flavor.

Tapping into
silent surges,
words with layers,
implying deeper meaning,
controlled yet passionate.
I see how we've strayed,
lost amidst our vulnerabilities.

An angel perches on my shoulder,
whispers into my inner ear,
sweet words of courage, patience, motivation,
"You've got this."
He's a constant presence,
Supporting me ceaselessly.

The bargaining chip,
to be authentic demands courage,
vulnerability risks rejection,
honesty and reflection,
not shame or deceit,
but truth in intention.

Embracing Complexity

Nothing is missing,
Is it normal
to feel dissatisfied?
to crave something better?
Nothing is tidy,
wrapped in glittery paper, tied with a bow.
As we scramble,
to unwrap the present and discover
It's not empty.
It holds
Contents.

Once,
I was showered with blessings,
of eternal vibration.
I entered the realm of love and acceptance,
blossomed with delicate petals of kindness.
It's a blessing filled with complexities.
Human nature abounds with stories.

Our perception of reality,
filtered through life's experiences,
while walking in other people's shoes,
we create optical illusions and call it normal.

The Daily Cocktail

The beverage can be a blend,
not bewildering,
sweet or savory,
vivid or transparent,
but always flavorful.

The days
morph into
forgotten trails of memories.
She gets lost in the intricacies of Stroke and Dementia.
Age, blunt force trauma,
ADHD, Autism, or total defeat.
She bleeds every day.

The bridge to recovery,
embraces the darkness
not as a nightmare
but as a comfort,
Rest.
In peace and tranquility,
worry less and have awe.

In the journey to heal,
she sips from the cup of resilience,
with each challenge, she grows stronger,
finding solace in the quiet moments,
resting in peace and tranquility,
no longer consumed by worry,
she discovers the beauty of life anew.

Alchemy

A diamond is a gem that undergoes a transformation through time and immense pressure, emerging as a radiant beauty with its unique carat weight. Without this journey, it's merely an unremarkable lump of rock. Our ego often seeks significance, yet we must acknowledge that we are but grains of sand on the vast shore of existence. Life and death coexist in a complex paradox, shaping the frequency of our existence. In this grand scheme, there are no true victims or coincidences; every aspect of our consciousness, whether conscious or unconscious, reflects like a mirror in the universe's cosmic light.

Our sense of humor varies, and differing perspectives can lead to conflicts. True peace often resides within the heart of conflict, amidst the various shades of gray that life presents. While grooves in our programming may bind us, sometimes for a lifetime, we must remember that help is often within our reach. We were created in the image of the divine, and it's crucial to take responsibility for our lives while remaining humble and grateful for heaven's grace. Finding peace and elevation in this journey is the ultimate goal, much like the alchemical process that turns raw materials into gold.

Reflecting on Our Wounds

The pain we endure,
affects those around us for sure.
Unaware, our words can be unkind,
like poison, they flow, leaving wounds inside.

Like daggers,
they pierce us deep carrying toxic strain,
leaving us scarred, but also more humane.
Our skin grows thicker, yet we silently bleed,
in our wounded hearts, the pain takes heed.

With hindsight, I now perceive,
the aftermath of wars we weave.
while humanity's swing of both chaos and grace,
I meditate on change, in our own defense.

Time

Infinity eludes through our grasp,
like grains in an hourglass,
it races, swift and unfeeling,
leaving us in its frenetic sprint.

Just yesterday, youthful and carefree,
today, the distant history already,
tomorrow, tomorrow, a fresh instant,
time progresses, inevitable and unwavering.

Let's seize every proffered moment,
live the present, relish the now,
for time, it lingers for no opening,
it transports us in its unending motion.

Let's sprint, waltz, adore without reservation,
before time appropriates them,
the cherished instants we protect,
for breath is exquisite, but time concludes.

Tunefulness

It's water, air, and also the ether's grace,
The wind, the rain, and winter's cold embrace.
It's night and darkness, it's dawn's soft glow,
Waiting and love, when you say "I love you" and I know.

It's tomorrow, today, and yesterday's track,
That piercing scream, the noise, and sometimes hellish black.
It's everything and nothing, filling all of space,
Especially when you leave, and I'm left to save face.

It's the "no" and the "yes," and the question "why?"
Time passing by, boredom, and moments of dread nearby.
It's the king, the prince, and also the plebs we meet,
Singing, feeling fear, and times of feeling weak.

It's the salt, the waves, and the vast, endless sea,
The sand's warm touch, and thirst in the desert's decree.
It's fear and death, intertwined with life's bright gleam,
Tears and laughter, and above all, the burning desire's beam.

It's the mother and child, it's the heartbeat's start,
Wheat fields, soaring birds, and the beauty of a flower's part.
It's the friend, the lover, and the cherished wife,
It's you, it's me, balancing on life's scale of strife

Dayspring

I walk along a trail one quiet night.
The world presents a sad and lonely sight.
A silver quilt of fog lies low, it seems.
All creatures look asleep with somber dreams.

A glow of red and gold comes from the East.
Giving my eyes a hopeful, splendid feast.
The songbirds welcome the arriving day.
The sun's warm rays has now melt the fog.

This scene reflects what happened in my life.
My days have long been filled with painful strife.
And paralyzing sadness through the years.
But now a shining ray of hope appears.

The shy gentle caress of the sun flare melts my heart.
My being has taken a new and hopeful start.
For peace and justice, let us plant a seed.
So that more happiness showers on those in need.

Verses of the Soul

These Poems...

Each verse, a window into my pain,
lacking joy or hues that entertain,
dull and devoid of any gain,
no fire, no warmth to sustain.

Cryptic poems, a puzzle to unfold,
my critique decrypts, stories untold,
holding sincerity as their gold,
guided by practice, they unfold.

Poems of a man, shrouded in shade,
who favored attack, not barricade,
choosing not to wait, nor evade,
rather than a victim, he'd cascade.

These verses paint a somber tableau,
authored by one with an iron woe,
a sole ruler, no one else to bestow,
over these lines, where emotions flow.

Subtle poems, with rhymes sometimes vain,
topics shift, like a fleeting train,
inspired by a world, often inane,
yet reflecting the human bane.

A poem, its syllables so pallid,
carrying burdens that seem valid,
tugging at hearts, leaving love squalid,
for those who embrace the torrid.

Poems of the night, in darkness they thrive,
when light escapes, they come alive,
deep within, their source does derive,
to that silent well, they quietly dive.

Whispers and poems of the past and the new,
dividing the false from the true,
an insurmountable wall that grew,
in their verses, life's intricate milieu.

Poems and tears, sadness like a charm,
in a world of violet and lavender to disarm,
infusing hues, lending it a sense of calm,
amidst despair's relentless alarm.

Poems, a world's orbit they represent,
in a realm often insincere, bent,
with my mind as their constant ascent,
transmitting messages, with intent.

Is it a poem or mere amnesia's grace,
words jumbled, lost in time's embrace,
or a society, stuck in heretical space,
where clarity struggles in this chase?

Revolutionary poems, with terror's prose,
repelling purists, as fear in them grows,
straying far from where righteousness flows,
always lost on paths no one else knows.

Sensory poetry, a world they unveil,
in their diverse meanings, they set sail,
characterized by their rhythmic trail,
these poems, like arteries, never frail.

As the Days Pass

As the days pass by!
And suddenly, we feel a great sorrow,
it seems to us that time should stop
or turn slowly in dark circles.
But the hours, the days,
they form an uninterrupted chain,
rising and falling like the waves of the sea,
engulfing each other
and carrying the boat of our life far,
far away from the islands of joy....
Oh, sadness!
Pure and true, you enter the soul,
you enter my flesh as well.

Oshun

Gentle raindrops fall,
dissolving mountaintops.
sunlight's rays, though subtly bright,
ignite the world with gentle light,
breathing life into the hive,
where bees thrive in harmony.

A peaceful design, we find,
can shift the hearts of humankind,
not only through force or violent push,
but by stirring thoughts to hush,
weak'ning the urge to harm or kill,
replacing it with love skill.

Oshun, in your somber grace,
you symbolize an ancient place,
A wisdom deep and truly old,
Your presence, like a story told,
A lovely flower, strength within,
When you say, "I'll go," it's akin
To shaking even the mightiest wall,
Leaving it defenseless to fall.

Your smile, a beacon, bright and kind,
Bringing peace to every mind,
You sow the seeds of calm release,
And in your wake, all conflicts cease.
You craft a world where tensions cease,
Where harmony finds its lasting lease.

The curves upon your face do trace
The gentle waves in a mountain's grace,
Your eyes beam like the morning sun,
Bringing joy to everyone.
Calm as the moon's soft silver gleam,
Reflecting in a tranquil stream.

Your voice, a friend's soothing grace,
Reveals your inner tranquil place,
Sweeter than the sweetest bird,
Its melodies, they all are heard.

Oshun,
Your hair, a waterfall so fine,
Threads of silk, in a graceful line.
Your hands, delicate and warm to hold,
Like summer sands, so smooth, so bold.

Oshun,
Your laughter fills my heart with cheer,
Your smile, a masterpiece so clear,
Can thaw the icy grip of rage,
Turning hatred's darkened page,
In your presence, anger wanes,
Forgiveness flows, and love remains.

Forgive me, please, my heart's desire,
For falling for you, I won't tire.
In your presence, life feels so true,
With you around, each day feels new.

The Demise of the Press

I mourn the demise of the press,
my pen decries the assault on freedom of expression,
everywhere be it on the streets of democracy,
or under dictatorship, voices are muzzled.

Reading is a puzzle for those unable to decipher events,
when the liberty to speak, hear, inquire,
and investigate is extinguished,
what remains but a succession of censorships?

Silencing the press is a crime against the people;
you see, a journalist can serve as a guiding light,
and without authentic, verifiable news, darkness shrouds society,
in today's complex systems, being informed has become a transgression.
Delivering news has transformed into misinforming,
we reside in an era of profuse informers,
with an abundance of information and knowledge at every turn, it seems,
yet, we are the most ill-informed public ever...

Lademonpolis 2050

The year is 2050, and I find myself immersed in contemplation, seated at Rosendal Café, in the heart of Lademonpolis, an enclave characterized by its dynamic and avant-garde spirit. Beyond the window, Innherretveien street′s bustling traffic weaves through the tapestry of my memories. I sit there, my hands cradling my chin, adrift in a sea of thoughts. Sometimes, beneath my reality, there's an intriguing surreal undertow.

A shadow dances along the veins of Lademonpolis, a district once called Lademoen back in the day. In Lamonpolis park, the dew heralds the arrival of a tentative warmth. Above, stars twinkle, and the first seagulls embark on their nocturnal journey, bearing messages of hope. The firmament bathes in the celestial ambrosia.

I belong to the generation of misfits, born into the zenith of technological prowess. Censorship casts a shadow over the vibrant thoughts expressed on social networks. The hieroglyphs on our screens synchronize with symbols that soothe our minds. Amidst this, a homeless man seeks shelter under the Trykkestallen tunnel, sometimes braving the cold, his cap offering little warmth. Can Lademonpolis, with its grandeur, ever extend a welcoming embrace to the homeless?

Time speeds by, and we must resist the urge to become ensnared in the relentless whirlwind of our unattainable pursuits. Whether one embraces it or not, Nyhuset, the wooden skyscraper, in all its majesty, watches over the sprawling nebula of Svartlamon city–a sanctuary of dignity and freedom. Behind this facade, graffiti celebrates an unbalanced joy. Where does this propensity for scaling walls lead us? To the walls of solitary laughter, bathed in the dim light of ambiguous tomorrows, promising fresh beginnings.

Today, I awoke early, the day unfolding leisurely. However, I chose to remain enveloped in the embrace of slumber, surrendering to the winter's darkness.

And so I remember, on the last radiant summer day, my mother departed from this world, right here in Lademonpolis. The circumstances were somber, and my father had foreseen it, even though they were together, yet apart. Her passing was abrupt, a tragic end at the hands of my other father, a peaceful slumber turned eternal rest.

Ironically, we had been preparing for my sister's wedding in Lademonpolis cathedral, the only church in town. A wedding that became a funeral, festivities turned to sorrow. The sun shone brightly that day, but our tears flowed unabated. Poverty weighed heavily upon our family. We laid my mother to rest with humility, as the evening descended quickly, and the Buran street, now deserted, grew darker.

Just a few days later, my father quickly sought solace in the arms of another woman, a younger one, from the Voldsminde suburb of Lademonpolis. For a while, pleasure masked his anxieties, but soon they returned to haunt him. He drowned himself in vices and addictions, slowly succumbing to a relentless disease that gnawed at his being.

Specialists dissected my father's body, and he was taken to the hospital. Any hope of survival vanished. The specialists used him as a valuable subject for their research. The day of his second burial approached. In keeping with his beliefs, he desired a proper funeral. We carried his coffin to Lademopolis Cemetery, another scorching day, another stroke of misfortune. Friends orchestrated the funeral, and we children felt detached from the ceremony. The cemetery seemed sinister, a place where the departed were forever erased from the memories of their descendants.

My mother's passing had left me grieving, but my father's death left me perplexed. It felt as though my life was poised to take a different course. To escape my somber responsibilities, I joined the ranks of those seeking solace, a world of decay that provided me with solace. The night suited my concealed face; it was a tranquil sea, a respite from the abyss of death.

My existence became a string of failures, my pursuit of nothingness a balm for my weary soul. Lademonpolis was where I learned about society, adopting a contemplative stance toward the world's events. My social circle revolved around anonymous cafes, gathering places for the marginalized, individuals with uncertain origins.

My family became a burden that I quickly grew weary of, for it obstructed my temporary liberation. A different kind of stimulant than the one I had sought so often offered me respite. Women intrigued me but failed to fulfill me, reflecting an unattainable happiness, an ever-varying mirage.

My wanderings led me to the enigmatic veiled woman, named as Amida, known as the dancer. Amida hailed from SING-SING in the very Lademonpolis erea too; of mysterious origin that intrigued and fascinated me. She remained elusive, like a chimera, forever distant, guiding me into a labyrinth of enchanted imprisonment. She was a marvel.

My family had noticed Amida's presence, a shadow lingering in the backdrop of my obscure existence. An unbreakable bond tied me to this mesmerizing dancer. Encounters with Amida liberated me from my stagnant despair, breathing new life into Lademonpolis. The family home began to feel stifling, suffocating my freedom. A different elixir became my refuge, offering stimulation rather than sedation.

I yearned to escape the confines of Lademonpolis, dreaming of unknown journeys and distant lands, for She herself came from afar–yeah, Amida from Lademonpolis.

It's the year 2050 in Lademonpolis, and from Rosendal cafe, I tread the path toward Mellomveien street, eternally seeking....Amida from Lademonpolis.

Alkhebulan

Yes, I remember, and
I will remember forever and always.
Innocence, peace, freedom, joy, all coexisted with the confusion
and the perfectly tamed disaster.
Despite the challenges that filled the world,
you did everything in your power to make me happy.
You were all I knew,
and the thought of a future without you was unimaginable.

Until the day the opportunity to join that long-desired stranger was offered to me.
There was no hesitation within me.
My body remained with you, but my mind wandered elsewhere.
I envisioned her as tall, beautiful, generous, welcoming,
always smiling, graceful, joyful, happy, and luxurious - everything you weren't.
Suddenly, you appeared old, ugly, poor, desolate, mean, dirty, unhappy,
and pitiful. All I desired was to bid you farewell.

Today,
it has been years since I've lived with that once longed-for stranger.
Yet, all I see in her is that you are deeply dear to my heart,
and I would give anything to relive moments with you.
I am nostalgic for your naturalness,
the joy that thrived amid chaos,
and the beauty that emerged from turmoil.
I long to see your long-dormant intelligence rise to its zenith.

Forgive me, my dear, for today I know better.
Forgive me, my Love, for the unknown revealed who you truly are.
Forgive me, my Angel, for I believed you were cursed,
but I now know you are blessed.
Forgive me, my treasure,
for I believed you were poor,
but your riches are still vast.
Forgive me, my heroine,
for I thought you were on the decline,
but I know it will take more than time to erase you from the map.

Forgive me, my beauty,
for today I know that "being black" is more a source of pride than a "curse."
Forgive me, my sweetness,
for I've seen that the only paradise on earth is indeed you.
Forgive me, my heart,
for I have utterly succumbed to your charm.
Forgive me, my sun, for today, day after day,
hour after hour, minute after minute,
second after second, I long for your warmth, which I inexorably miss.

Tomorrow, it won't be easy,
but I am profoundly convinced that it will be your time to shine.
You have preserved that charming naturalness
that attract many admirers.
Above all, keep a watchful eye on the painful lessons
you've been taught by a past as distant as it is present,
so you'll never be deceived again; especially not by the allure of decayed wealth.

Oh! Khemet, my Africa!
I would love to see you finally, one day, in your rightful place as the queen of princesses.
Oh! Alkhebulan, brave Africa!
How many mothers would still be able to smile after losing so many offspring?
Oh dzimba dzemabwe, land of my ancestors.
It's time to finally benefit from the products derived from your own seed.
Oh Mandé, the land of people of integrity
How can you still accept that they dare to demand debts from you
after your children were taken into slavery and stripped of all your minerals?
Oh Abbysinya, youthfull Africa!
We must no longer, we cannot let our "mother" live in such conditions.

Let's stop ignoring our "mother's" desperate cries.
Let's stop waiting for others, most of whom are responsible for
or have contributed to this disaster - Mafi.
Oh Nubia, sweet Africa
Alkhebulan,
Let grow.

Alkebulan,

Yesterday, I remember, and I will cherish forever and always.
Innocence, peace, freedom, joy, they all thrived amid the chaos,
and the perfectly tamed disaster.
Despite the challenges that filled the world,
you did everything in your power to bring me happiness.
You were my only world,
and the thought of a future without you was unimaginable.

Until the day the opportunity to join that long-desired stranger was presented to me.
There was no hesitation within my heart.
My body remained with you, but my mind wandered elsewhere.
I pictured her as tall, beautiful, generous, and welcoming,
always smiling, graceful, joyful, happy, and luxurious - everything you were not.
Suddenly, you appeared aged, unsightly, impoverished, desolate, unkind, soiled, unhappy,
and pitiable. All I yearned for was to bid you farewell.

Today,
it has been years since I've shared life with that once longed-for stranger.
Yet, all I see in her is that you are deeply embedded in my heart,
and I would give anything to relive moments with you.
I long for your authenticity,
the joy that thrived amid the chaos,
and the beauty that emerged from turmoil.
I yearn to witness your dormant intelligence rise to its zenith.

Forgive me, my dear, for today I see the truth.
Forgive me, my Love, for the unknown revealed your true essence.
Forgive me, my Angel, for I thought you were cursed,
but now I know you are blessed.
Forgive me, my treasure,
for I thought you were destitute,
but your riches remain vast.
Forgive me, my heroine,
for I believed you were in decline,

but I know it will take more than time to erase you from the map.
Forgive me, my beauty,
for today I know that "being black" is a source of pride, not a "curse."
Forgive me, my sweetness,
for I've seen that the only paradise on earth is indeed you.
Forgive me, my heart,
for I have completely surrendered to your charm.
Forgive me, my sun, for today, day after day,
hour after hour, minute after minute,
second after second, I long for your warmth, which I dearly miss.

Tomorrow, it won't be easy,
but I am profoundly convinced that it will be your time to shine.
You have preserved that enchanting authenticity
that draws many admirers.
Above all, keep a vigilant eye on the painful lessons
you've learned from a past as distant as it is present,
so you'll never be deceived again, especially not by the allure of decaying wealth.

Oh! Khemet, my Africa!
I yearn to see you finally, one day, in your rightful place as the queen of princesses.
Oh! Alkebulan, valiant Africa!
How many mothers would still find the strength to smile after losing so many offspring?
Oh dzimba dzemabwe, land of my ancestors.
It's time to reap the rewards from the seeds you've sown.
Oh Mandé, the land of people of integrity!
How can you still accept the audacity of debt demands,
after your children were taken into slavery, and your minerals were plundered?
Oh Abbysinya, youthful Africa!
We must no longer, we cannot allow our "mother" to endure such conditions.

Let's cease to ignore our "mother's" desperate pleas.
Let's refrain from waiting for others, many of whom are complicit in
or have contributed to this calamity - Maafa.

Oh Nubia, sweet Rugari, Kivu ´s bride
Nyragongo volcanoes , land of fertility

Alkebulan,
Let us thrive and grow.
Oh! Ruwenzori mon amour.
I will always mount your heart.

Woman of Timbuktu

Enchanting as the desert that surrounds you,
Your crimson silk from Syria veils a precious gem,
A gift of dignity and profound respect,
You embody the essence of enlightenment.

Mystical amidst the mirage-filled winds,
Through your unwavering devotion,
You stand as the bastion of your tribe,
Your mere presence ignites the fires within our souls.

You, the songstress,
Witnessing these unbelievers,
Who have encroached upon your freedom,
Observing these exploiters,
Insha'Allah, surely you merit a revolution.

Restless Night

Survival is the everyday's plea,
Life in the present, the heart's decree.
Tomorrow's certainty, the specter of death,
The shine fades, stealing our breath.

In waters deep, tiny fish do roam,
Birds soar high, seeking a home.
Meanwhile, death's shadow does surround,
May the butler serve honey, sweet and profound.

Rumble! O fury of our majestic peaks,
Drown out the drumbeat, the fear that seeks.
River flows through our valleys wide,
Tasteless sweat from the earth, we bide.
A winding course reflects the alley's grace,
Where the sunflower hums, in a tranquil space.

Unconscious beings, both woman and man,
Facing tomorrow's fate, as only mortals can.
In the seeds of their deeds, their fame will sow,
Truth revealed, in the afterlife's glow.
Speak to me now, ancestral spirits near,
Guide my soul, dispel doubt and fear.

In order or chaos, reveal my destined place,
To my wandering mind, grant solace and grace.
Without respite, I wander, lost and forlorn,
Welcome me, siren, with a melodious horn.
Nymphs may shun, preferring flesh not bone,
Yet I persevere, though I'm all alone.

My body crumbles, in this nightmarish strife,
I scream, I shake, grappling with life.
What is this nightmare that strangles with might,
In its tentacles, I yearn for the light?

Untitled

Gloomy life's gift
Yet denying death's release too
In shadows we dwell

Handing Over

Do they grasp the essence of it all?
Even if I were a fruit, a berry, an eggplant tall.
Or just a stone, lost in vast terrain,
Invisible, like a dancer in the desert's grain.

War, oh war, relentless strife,
I see you lurking, threatening life.
Everywhere I turn, you stand so bold,
In dreams, you haunt me, your stories told.

I've shed the illusions, left them behind,
In silence, I dwell, a grapefruit of the mind.
Ny false privileges crumble, they matter no more,
Abandoned, I stand, on life's barren shore.

Today, they claim to promote democracy's light,
Yet neglect's abyss, bureaucratic might.
Desire's demise, a mournful tune, .
They fail to see, the deep suffering,
In the land's forsaken, in hearts that weep.
Handing over, this world's endless fight,
In the silence of night, we search for the light.

Butterfly

Come, swim with me beneath
the moon, in the night's dewdrops.
Moonlight.
Beneath us,
we walk barefoot on dewy grass,
sticking to our feet.

Fly, magical butterfly,
Fly in the moonlight.
Your power! Alien, yet so familiar to me.
Loved by the moon, come bathe with me.
Lead me into your sparkling sea of stars
Butterfly, the daughter of light and freedom
Smile, leap, and dance
Under the moon's glow

You leave a gentle hue in the air, a hope
My beloved, float, dream, embrace me,
as you graps the night's light,
Because you are the glittering queen of the night.

Dark, yet shining
The twilight's emerald Butterfly,
fly in the luminescence
Dance in the moonlight
Naked, loved, you are the lyre of the earth,
nature's perfume, my sublime dance

O! Butterfly in the fearless radiance,
you are my wish, bathed in tender blessings
Dance, my butterfly, my hope,
my freedom, my dream,
the deepest desire of my soul.

It is dawn

It is dawn as I curl up in my cold crib
I am cramped in this crumbling freezing world
It is dawn as I grasp the first radiance of an indifferent sun
In the middle of the crowd, I feel strangely narrower

In this collapsing realm
I cast aside your code
Nor to be compliant
If to get into the norm we must put on suits
the flare that consumes my soul
It's to learn how to be a human being without anything distorting my spirit

Far from your cadence
I dance against the grain to raise my level of consciousness
It doesn't matter if tomorrow I must depart
I would have lived the present

How do you see the future?
What our children will inherit from us
These youth who are living increasingly on the margins of our society

How ready are you to be brought down?
I need a larger vision
I want to resist by always moving forward against the odds
to be me despite the dress code

Blasphemer of the first day
The poet words are to heal the injured soul
even if this does not atone for all the world filthy misdeeds
I cry for justice
I bring a prayer of hope to humankind
as they race against the clock

It is dawn as I curl up in my cold crib
certainly, I had a glass too much
I am cramped in this crumbling freezing world
It is dawn as I grasp the first radiance of an indifferent sun
In the middle of the crowd, I feel strangely narrower
I am but a human by chance thrown on this swirling planet

Dinanga, the Ark of Refuge

Eighteen days since the ship began its voyage toward the distant capital town of Kin-Malebo;
On the majestic river Congo; sailing slowly and hesitantly on the vicious liquid leaving behind the foretold fall of a regime in disarray.
We have tamped everything down under the bags of cassava; the life conditions are unimaginable on the barges.

Solitude!

When the shadow of the night appears, the torrential equatorial rains choose to flagellate us with no leniency. During the day and under the torrid sun, the *tsetse* flies bite us relentlessly with no mercy.
Kraaaak! Suddenly, once again, trapped into a bank of sand. The roaring of the engine hangs over our weakened heart.

The Dinanga vessel is exhausted.

Drifting over five hundred kilometers from Boyoma city, nearing Lisala the birth town of the eagle of *Kawele* palace, *Mobutu Sese Seko.*
The weakened Dinanga has thrown itself in the submerged sandbank. Piled up with the merchandises, the passengers are grieving... Yeah! Weeping and mourning such is our quotidian burden on this haunted ark of refuge. The malevolent has arrived. One or two departed per day. Life is obscure. The number of effected is yet to be known: A death from dysentery, a death from misery. The time is suspended, days have passed. Without fuel, we are stuck helpless into the wet sand in the middle of the serpent river, Congo river.
Meanwhile, things fall apart

In front of us, in Kinshasa, the leopard has fled... Moreover, behind us the kadogo-child-soldiers have dismembered the giant one, *Zaïre...*

The light of our faith dissolves leaving us on the moist island of misfortune.

We are but a sample of what people from all corners of the land are enduring.

Grief –Abandonment–
Now among the bags of manioc, under the trap of wealth, a new victim shies away.
A friend, a sister and brother, who yesterday was well full of hope and dreams vanishes today.
While currently in my reminiscence, his face remains forever etched into my spirit:
A man who fights to survive; alone, a refugee on the boat, Attacked by diseases... His heart wants to let go ...

– Along the River Congo; memory in the whispering winds –

Intrigue of the Heart

Step into our hearts,
Wide open and beautifully alive,
Step into our hearts,
Mysterious as the pages of a book,
Within, love has sown its roses,
Yet beware, for hatred surrounds them with thorns,
Beside goodness, evil ever lurks,
For morality and ethics, we must embrace both.

In our hearts, coursing more than just blood,
You'll find boundless joy, devoid of sorrow,
Yonder, our dreams flourish in every direction,
These chambers house countless prayers,
Innocence, abandoned since our youth,
And our most exquisite, idyllic joys reside therein,
Ignore our haunting fears, they shall one day be stilled.

Be cautious not to approach their boundaries,
On the other side, weepings and resentments lie,
Shattered hearts and festering wounds,
Stay with me, as one would in a captivating book,
Fear not, our hearts are intoxicated,
Drunk with radiance, bestowing happiness,
Know that when I lose myself in a book,
I rediscover myself, refined and renewed.

Enter our hearts, where the journey begins,
They are enigmatic like the pages of a book,
Judge us not by our cover,
The door merely marks the start of our dwelling,
Hidden treasures you shall never glimpse,
Not even in our most heartfelt smiles,
Only in the depths of our convoluted hearts.

Embrace silence, a tranquil hush,
Listen intently, hear your own listening,
Can you discern the celestial blue melody?

Listen again! Yes, listen! The poet is not mad,
It's poetry that dances on the edge of reason,
Infatuated with beauty, wherever it may be found,
Enthralled when perfection grazes our souls.

The doors of our hearts won't remain ajar,
Forever open they cannot be,
Thus, make the gesture that speaks of faith,
Before they close, before they unveil our essence,
And know that our hearts are intoxicated,
Inebriated with light, offering boundless joy,
For within the pages of a book,
I lose myself, Only to rediscover a better version of me

Quest Beyond the Elements

In the silky cocoons of clouds,
Amidst the muffled breath of storms,
Within the sudden spark of lightning's shroud,
In the gray and clear fog's elusive forms,
I'll seek for you

In the emerald hollows of ocean's waves,
Across the restless wandering sea,
In the ebb and flow where mystery paves,
With moored lighthouses guiding me,
I'll seek for you, through endless days.

Through fields and meadows, dreams unfold,
In the plantations of reveries, we'll roam,
Upon the tops of trees, stories untold,
In the intoxicated roots, our hearts find home,
I'll seek for you, a bond untold.

Amongst mountain rocks and colors so wide,
Through freezing rain and fog's disguise,
Amongst the waves of the screaming tide,
In nature's grandeur, our love will rise,
I'll seek for you, forever by my side.

In torrents' rush and waterfalls' grace,
Along the winding rivers' gentle flow,
By dams and ponds, in each tranquil place,
As time ebbs and flows, our love will grow,
I'll seek for you, in every embrace.

Beyond the expanding universes' vast array,
Past merging dreams and stars up high,
Through arches of rainbows in the sky's display,
I'll seek for you, where love can never die,

Beyond horizons and expectations, come what may.
Through forgiven wanderings and friendships so strong,

In this unyielding quest, I'll persist and renew,
For in the end, where we truly belong,
In your arms, my love, I will find you.

The Birth of the Sun

My tears are the line of my novel
The characters are rigid
Stiff and ready to act in my cynical scenario
I am the milestones of all misfortunes
And mischances that hunt the running-gods in the firmament –
My splendour reaches the stars in the immeasurable spaces
And always declines as I reach "Isis"
giving birth to "Apollo"

Harmony's Cry

Africa, a land of plenty they say,
Yet hunger's shadow looms, taking lives away.
In ubuntu's embrace, none left in despair,
Shared resources, a bond we used to wear.

A fundamental option, for the poor and the old,
Community's heart, in stories often told.
Policies must change, for fairness we plead,
Sustainable development, the world's deepest need.

Wars over minerals have left scars so deep,
Peace and tranquility, a treasure to keep.
But who is our foe, in this endless strife?
War is blind, it knows no face or life.

In these trying times, division runs wild,
Bigotry, ethnocentrism, the world beguiled.
Rich and poor, the gap ever wide,
Disease, strife, inequality on this ride.

Our common enemy, let's unite and see,
Poverty, disease, hunger, and lack of decree.
Clean water, pollution, problems we share,
In harmony's cry, let's rise, let's care.

Freedom´s plea

In a realm cloaked in enigmatic restraints, where cryptic mandates shroud its people in the shadow of prejudice, discontent reigns supreme.

For humanity, by its very nature, yearns to unfurl its wings and soar in the boundless expanse of liberty. All treasures and knowledge should be within the grasp of each soul, unfettered by the shackles of wealth's insatiable lust for personal dominion.

Should you find yourself ensnared within such a society, a wanderer on the outskirts may beckon you, whispering secrets of liberation elsewhere. A radical confrontation with the core of this enigma may be deemed necessary.

But let us tread with care, for violence, the ancient dance of conquerors and conquered, merely trades one yoke for another, one set of obligations for the next.

In the tapestry of human relations, those devoid of love have grown archaic, mere remnants of an antiquated era. Thus, contemplate departure from this realm, leave it behind in search of a fresher dawn.

Untitled

In a world where voices cry,
"Here, here!" we must comply.
Hear, hear the tale of N.G.O's,
And N.P.O's with noble throes.

They've embraced the elite's grand scheme,
Superstructures in their wildest dream.
Mimicking, they strive to be,
Or sometimes stumble, as we see.

With lesser checks and balances,
Accountability in tiny chances.
Let's hope they tread with care and grace,
To serve humanity in this vast space

Brave Despair

In a world where the devil's hand bestows a rose,
City flames ignite as bluecoats deal with a civil blow.
It's all quite daunting, yet I fear no more,
Worldwide, allure in spirits, women left ashore.

Children blend weed in rolled tobacco wraps,
Jealousy's venom, more lethal than cancer's traps.
Employers blur lines 'twixt labor and chains,
Be honest, they say, or embrace theft's dark lanes.

Welcome to this brave new world's parade,
While prisons beckon, arms open, no goodbye.
Half a century's toil, parents strive in vain,
Peace lies deep in an abyss of endless pain.

Life wears a shroud of melancholy's haze,
Evening prayers, hope's beacon in this maze.
In my homeland, rights for elites are the norm,
While hunger's shadow casts its cruel swarm.

As famine whispers on the horizon's ledge,
Pandemics, wars, guns, and disaster's sting,
Hatred multiplies, chaos' dissonant ring.

This world, indeed, bears a chilling face,
Politicians' scandals, a never-ending chase.
As minors roam free through the digital expanse,
Shutdowns and quarantines, yet profits enhance.
In A new world, or so it may seem.
Exhausted from marching and protesting's cry,
Still, I pursue justice, under the same sky.

Trials

A blend of joy and sorrow entwined,
The past, with a cold grin, haunts the future's design.
Today, this parting pains our hearts so,
Despite the open and encouraging hands we know.

As time marches forward, tears have been shed,
Witnessing this union unravel, fills us with dread.
Our shared laughter, now a tapestry of memories,
A remembrance of an era threatened by uncertainties.

Nevertheless, this story that binds us may seem frail,
Destined for potential oblivion, we set sail.
Yet, we'll remain connected, striving to stay intact,
For every journey endures change, and that's a fact.

Stepping over the threshold, burdens held tight,
We know, for certain, we won't see each other tonight.
Like a procession, we depart in tears today,
With heavy hearts, we'll safeguard what hope may stay.

May the cries within our souls serve as our redemption,
Indeed, this new journey affects us all, no exemption.
Sadness cannot be contained, it's a force so true,
Who can conjure a brighter fate for us as trials ensue?

Poetical Morning

I walk along a trail one quiet night.
The world presents a sad and lonely sight.
A silver quilt of fog lies low, it seems.
All creatures look asleep with somber dreams.

A glow of red and gold comes from the East
Giving my eyes a hopeful, splendid feast.
The songbirds welcome the arriving day.
The sun's warm rays now melt the fog away.

This scene reflects what happened in my life.
My days have long been filled with painful strife
And paralyzing sadness through the years.
But now a shining ray of hope appears.

The shy gentle caress of the sun flare melts my heart.
My life has taken a new and hopeful start.
For peace and justice let us plant a seed.
So that more happiness showers on those in need.

Longing

Above the surface of the basin,
The elements are calm and amiable
Lost in the gardens of my imagination
And while on the horizon,
The ray of the sun is slowly fading incessantly downhill.
From my balcony,
I marvel at the august somber and decorated lake

Soon the swirling shadow of the hills will merge into the sky
And the evocative songs of the fishermen
Will devour the monotonous melody of nightingales.

Soon the heaven strewn with stars
Perpetuating harmony and serenity
Until the dawn of another day and other wonders.
O! Motherland far yet so close to my bosom

You challenge your profaners from there and elsewhere,
And you offer to those whose flesh feeds at your breast
Such moments of escape into your bright future!
You! My longing, thus the gods shaped you: peaceful and splendid

Old Beauty

A flight of times,
A flight of petals,
The wind blows,
The perfect fades Charms vanish.

Endless smartness,
Eternal sensuality,

O wild beauty!
The world adores your youthfulness,
We celebrate the death of time.

Fatima

Fatima, the dreamer,
Past joy of passions,
In your new family,
You, so young,
Are now the smokes of fury,
And behind you, the rumors.

Fatima, the youngest girl,
Sits, thinking,
Stricken by the fruit of romance;
Paths, which had seemed so clear.

Fatima, the innocent,
In the middle of your earthly voyage,
Only regrets.
Living with Okoth, your spouse so poor.
But after carnal leisure and affection–
The end of tenderness, a doubtful future.

Fatima, woman of uncertainty,
So heavy is the decision;
Your needs are rarely met,
Two children pull at your skirt,
And precious is the life in your womb
Yet no worth for Okoth.

Fatima, mother of misery,
Coldness is your kitchen,
Insufficient is your feeling, your trust.
Your purse is empty.
Poor Fatima.
Your brother is poverty, your sister neglect.

Fatima, married so young,
Woman of courage,
Often, the indecent proposition.
Finally, the reluctant sigh of agreement–
You enter the dimness of cluttered rooms

Fatima, wise adulteress,
On the alter of undesirable desire, you are immolated.
The sons of debauchery suck at the breasts of your dignity.
Your body is ravaged as prey,
Providing the milk of erotic decadence
To satisfy the thirst of man's uncontrolled passions.

Fatima, peddler of flesh,
Your being, a tortured sacrifice,
Your heart forced into loveless love,
But your duty you're doing, your self-abandonment,
Is shamefully endured for love and survival of family.

Fatima, woman of thought,
When sun is warm caressing the earth,
You dutifully care for and feed your children.
The price of your sacrifice
Is fear frozen in your thoughts:
Perhaps the rust of your life nears its end.

Fatima, solitary woman, Your spouse so quiet,
The experience of mutual humiliation,
The hurried pain-filled glances.
Alone you remain, alone you are.

Fatima, ghost of my towns,
You find her nightly on pavements,
Cold of soul, waiting for sinners of darkness.

From Kampala to Dar-es-Salaam, her spectre is seen;
From Kinshasa to Burundi, her phantom is present;
In Kigali, in Nairobi, the festering wound of society persists.

Fatima, know your dream:
To be clothed with dignity,
To be acknowledged as wife and mother.

My impassioned desire for you:
That you arise from the gutters of untold cities
To the heights of true womanhood and acceptability
With sustenance and shelter for you and for those you love.

Second Dimension

Near his table rests a glass of water;
Through his window he glances at passerby;
He observes and always waits, waits, waits.

Bitterness nourishes his being;
Subjected to misunderstandings
And false airs of 'people'
He is a prisoner.

He sits, hands cupped around his chin
Solemnly thinking.
In his dreaming, his spirits escape
The world of hardships
And travel in the expanses of the
Wild blue sky.

He leans on his table, half worried, half-contented.
In this place of his there is no compassion;
Evil prowls around its prey;
Rancor sings its melody of morning.

A stranger to his land,
He melancholically sips from his glass—
A sip of freedom.

Marginalized and needy,
Very far is the wind of liberty blowing for him
He is a clandestine, always without address,
Not a nomad, but a recluse in the midst of humanity.

In his unbroken crystal enclosure
He follows the echoes of his silent screams.
A rock of madness, only solitude answers him.

He startles!
His heart rapidly beats!
He rises from his bed!
Ah! It's only a nightmare!

Mmap New African Poets Series

If you have enjoyed *Best New African Poets 2023 Anthology*, consider these other fine books in the ***Mmap New African Poets Series*** from *Mwanaka Media and Publishing:*

I Threw a Star in a Wine Glass by Fethi Sassi
Best New African Poets 2017 Anthology by Tendai R Mwanaka and Daniel Da Purificacao
Logbook Written by a Drifter by Tendai Rinos Mwanaka
Mad Bob Republic: Bloodlines, Bile and a Crying Child by Tendai Rinos Mwanaka
Zimbolicious Poetry Vol 1 by Tendai R Mwanaka and Edward Dzonze
Zimbolicious Poetry Vol 2 by Tendai R Mwanaka and Edward Dzonze
Zimbolicious: An Anthology of Zimbabwean Literature and Arts, Vol 3 by Tendai Mwanaka
Under The Steel Yoke by Jabulani Mzinyathi
Fly in a Beehive by Thato Tshukudu
Bounding for Light by Richard Mbuthia
Sentiments by Jackson Matimba
Best New African Poets 2018 Anthology by Tendai R Mwanaka and Nsah Mala
Words That Matter by Gerry Sikazwe
The Ungendered by Delia Watterson
Ghetto Symphony by Mandla Mavolwane
Sky for a Foreign Bird by Fethi Sassi
A Portrait of Defiance by Tendai Rinos Mwanaka
Zimbolicious: An Anthology of Zimbabwean Literature and Arts, Vol 4 by Tendai Mwanaka and Jabulani Mzinyathi
When Escape Becomes the only Lover by Tendai R Mwanaka
ويَسهَرُ اللَّيلُ عَلَى شَفَتي...وَالغَمَام by Fethi Sassi
A Letter to the President by Mbizo Chirasha
This is not a poem by Richard Inya
Pressed flowers by John Eppel
Righteous Indignation by Jabulani Mzinyathi:
Blooming Cactus by Mikateko Mbambo
Rhythm of Life by Olivia Ngozi Osouha
Travellers Gather Dust and Lust by Gabriel Awuah Mainoo
Chitungwiza Mushamukuru: An Anthology from Zimbabwe's Biggest Ghetto Town by Tendai Rinos Mwanaka

Zimbolicious: An Anthology of Zimbabwean Literature and Arts, Vol 5 by Tendai Mwanaka
Because Sadness is Beautiful? by Tanaka Chidora
Of Fresh Bloom and Smoke by Abigail George
Shades of Black by Edward Dzonze
Best New African Poets 2020 Anthology by Tendai Rinos Mwanaka, Lorna Telma Zita and Balddine Moussa
This Body is an Empty Vessel by Beaton Galafa
Between Places by Tendai Rinos Mwanaka
Best New African Poets 2021 Anthology by Tendai Rinos Mwanaka, Lorna Telma Zita and Balddine Moussa
Zimbolicious: An Anthology of Zimbabwean Literature and Arts, Vol 6 by Tendai Mwanaka and Chenjerai Mhondera
A Matter of Inclusion by Chad Norman
Keeping the Sun Secret by Mariel Awendit
سِجلٌ مَكتُوبٌ لتَائهٍ by Tendai Rinos Mwanaka
Ghetto Blues by Tendai Rinos Mwanaka
Zimbolicious: An Anthology of Zimbabwean Literature and Arts, Vol 7 by Tendai Rinos Mwanaka and Tanaka Chidora
Best New African Poets 2022 Anthology by Tendai Rinos Mwanaka and Helder Simbad
Dark Lines of History by Sithembele Isaac Xhegwana
a sky is falling by Nica Cornell
Death of a Statue by Samuel Chuma
Along the way by Jabulani Mzinyathi
Strides of Hope by Tawanda Chigavazira
Young Galaxies by Abigail George
Coming of Age by Gift Sakirai
Mother's Kitchen and Other Places by Antreka. M. Tladi
Soon to be released

https://facebook.com/MwanakaMediaAndPublishing/